How Animals Communicate

Written by Jenny Feely
Series Consultant: Linda Hoyt

WorldWise
Content-based Learning

Contents

Chapter 1
Animal communication

All animals can send messages. They can communicate. They use sound, movement, colour and smells such as their natural body scent to communicate with each other.

Most animals communicate with animals of their own kind, which helps them to survive. Animals also need to understand the way other **species** act to help them to stay alive.

Scientists study how animals communicate. They believe that some animals may make sounds that always mean the same thing, almost like words. For example, they have observed that some kinds of monkeys make one sound to warn that a snake is near, and a different sound to warn of an eagle. But scientists still do not understand many things about how and why animals communicate.

People and language

Humans have the most **complex** communication systems of any living things. This is because they can use **language**. Language is any system of symbols that are used to communicate meaning. These symbols can be sounds (including words), body movements and print. There are at least 6,800 languages in the world.

How do animals communicate?

Different animals communicate in different ways. They may:

- make sounds
- use colour
- give off smells
- move in different ways
- touch each other
- use chemicals
- use **body language**
- use light

Why do animals communicate?

Animals communicate to:

- find food
- warn about dangers
- show affection
- find a mate
- make a rival leave
- defend their territory
- scare a **predator** away

Wolves use body language, smell and sound to communicate. The wolf on the left is showing the other wolf that it is the boss.

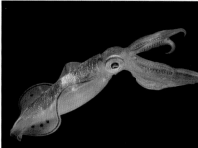

Squid use colour to communicate. A squid changes colour quickly to show it is ready to mate.

Horses use sound, touch and body language to communicate. Horses touch their muzzles to show affection.

Bees use movement to communicate. The bee in the middle dances to show other bees in its hive where to find nectar and pollen.

Deer use body language and movement to communicate. When deer flick their tails, they are telling others in their herd that danger is near.

Whales use sound and movement to communicate. They leap out of the water to show other whales that they are big and strong and would make a good mate.

Getting the message across

What are they saying?	How are they saying it?	
Go away!	This wolf growls and bares its teeth to scare other animals away.	
I like you.	These elephants are showing affection for each other by touching.	
Look at me. I'd be a good mate.	The male fiddler crab has one large claw and one small one. It waves its large claw to attract a mate.	
Danger!	This kangaroo thumps its back legs on the ground to warn others in its mob of danger.	
There's food here.	Chimpanzees make different calls to tell other members of their group that they have found food.	

Find out more

Many animals such as alligators, elephants and dogs produce tears. Once, people thought this was because they were sad. Is this true? Find out why animals shed tears.

Birds often sing to tell other birds to stay out of their territory.

Choose one of the animals from page 6 or 7. Find out more information about how and what your chosen animal communicates.

Lions rub their heads together, and hum and groan to show that they are friendly.

Male peacocks show that they have the most beautiful tails so that they are more likely to attract females.

Meerkats take turns to watch for predators. They then give a warning bark to their group.

When an ant finds food, it puts down a chemical trail to tell the other ants where the food is.

Try this

Try to communicate these messages to a partner without using any words:

Go away!

DANGER

There's food here.

Chapter 2

Sending messages

The ways animals send messages differ from **species** to species.
In this chapter, we look at how colour and electricity are used by
certain animals to communicate.

Cuttlefish rapidly change colour to communicate.

Colourful cuttlefish

Cuttlefish are strange-looking sea animals that spend much of
their time hunting and hiding near the ocean floor. They can
change the colour and look of their skin. This helps them to find
food, hide from **predators** and find a mate.

Most of the time, male and female cuttlefish look the same as each other. They both have a **mottled** pattern on their skin. But when the mating season comes around, male cuttlefish put on an amazing show. They give one message to the female cuttlefish nearby and a different message to other males.

They change the side of their body closest to the female to grey while at the same time showing a zebra-striped pattern (on the other side) to the males. The female cuttlefish remains mottled until she is ready to mate when she changes her skin to grey.

Find out more

Find out about other animals that change colour and why.

This cuttlefish has changed colour to hide itself on the seabed.

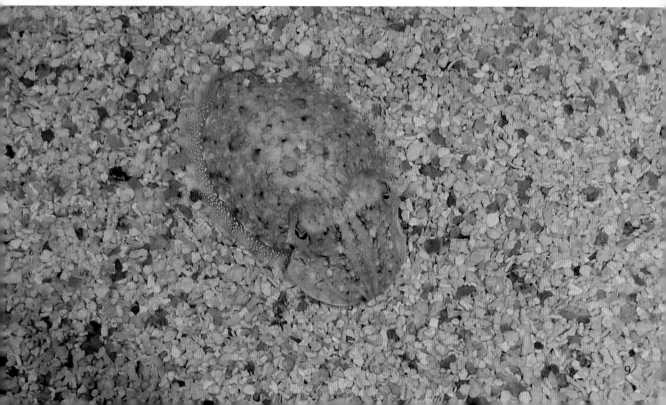

Once a female signals that she is ready, the male cuttlefish compete to win the chance to mate with her. They flash stronger colours and may even push or bite each other. Eventually, one male will win the contest, and the others will show that they are beaten by swimming away and returning to the usual mottled pattern.

The zebra pattern can be clearly seen on the male cuttlefish.

The male that wins the contest uses touch and movement to communicate with the female. The male may stroke her with his tentacles or blow bubbles onto her while slowly swimming away. The female shows she accepts him by opening her tentacles to the male as he swims back to her. Then they mate.

▼ This male cuttlefish is making a basket shape with his tentacles and showing a zebra pattern, which means it is looking for a mate.

Did you know?

Cuttlefish can change colour in less than a second by tightening or relaxing muscles that control **cells** on the surface of their skin. These cells are filled with red, yellow and black colours that are easily seen when the muscles tighten the cells. When the cells are relaxed, the colours almost disappear. The cuttlefish changes colour by changing which cells are relaxed or tightened.

Weakly electric fish often live in muddy waters where they cannot see far ahead. These fish give off small amounts of electricity to enable them to "see" where they are going and to find food. They can sense changes in the electrical field caused by other animals, and this enables them to sense the location of these animals. The electricity is given off by organs at the end of their bodies, and the receptor organs near their mouth pick up the signals from other weakly electric fish.

When a weakly electric fish swims near another of its kind, the weakly electric fish picks up the electrical signals of that fish. This tells the weakly electric fish the size and species of the fish and whether it is male or female.

Some kinds of weakly electric fish live in groups. In these groups, one male will be the **dominant** fish that gets to **fertilise** the eggs laid by all the females in the group.

The black ghost knife fish is a weakly electric fish that lives in the Amazon River.

Weakly electric fish:
- are usually nocturnal, which means that they are mostly active at night
- are found in fresh water in Central and South America, as well as in Africa
- emit about one volt of electricity, which would hurt a human, should they touch one accidentally

If another male fish wants to be dominant, it changes its electrical signal to match that of the dominant male. This often leads to a battle where the two fish stay locked jaw to jaw for a whole night until one fish wins. The winner will then be the dominant male until it loses to another fish.

Some weakly electric fish also communicate about mating. Females establish territories where they lay eggs. The dominant male fish will mate only with the female with the best territory. This female becomes the dominant female.

When ready to mate, the female hangs among the plants, and the male gives out 60–80 electrical signals a minute. These sound like chirps, and encourage the female to lay her eggs. Once she has done this, she chirps quietly, which is a signal for the male to fertilise the eggs.

◀ Electric eels are strongly electric fish.
▼ Strongly electric fish such as the electric catfish produce enough electricity to kill prey.

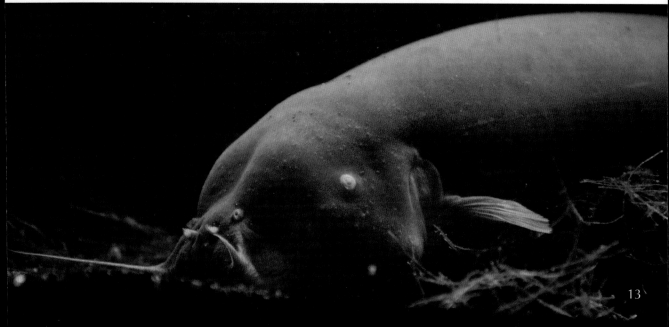

Chapter 3

Studying animal communication

Elephants

Cynthia Moss

Since 1972, Cynthia Moss has led a team of researchers studying elephants in the Amboseli National Park in Kenya, in Africa. During this time, Moss has collected information about more than 3,000 elephants. This is the largest study of elephants in their natural **habitat** ever done.

Moss and her team have collected information about elephant births and deaths in the park during this time. She has taken detailed notes about where elephants have been seen, and has recorded and analysed elephant behaviour. Moss has created records that identify each of the elephants in the park. She also has records that show how the elephants are related.

Amboseli National Park is in Kenya. In this park, elephants roam freely, protected from poachers who would kill them for their ivory tusks.

Moss has discovered that elephants live in family groups made up of related female elephants and their calves. Male adult elephants visit the herd from time to time to mate or to **socialise**. Elephant families work together in many ways, including defending the herd, finding food and looking after calves.

She has identified more than 168 different ways elephants communicate with each other.

Moss's work has enabled people to understand much more about elephant communication and behaviour. She hopes that if people understand elephants, they will be more likely to protect their habitat, and ensure their survival in the wild.

Did you know?

Scientists studying elephants collect information by:

- following them and observing their behaviour
- taking photos
- making audio and video recordings
- fitting some elephants with electronic collars.

What would collecting such information tell the scientists about how the elephants communicate?

How elephants communicate

The research done by Moss and her team has shown that elephants communicate using sound, movement, smell and touch.

Types of communication

Sound	Touch
How	**How**
Elephants use their voices and trunks to make many different sounds to communicate with each other. These include: • low rumbling sounds • screams • high trumpeting sounds • barks • snorts • roars	• Elephants touch each other with their trunks, ears, tusks, feet, tails or even their whole bodies to communicate. • An elephant's trunk may stroke another elephant to reassure or show affection. It may also show aggression by slapping or blocking another elephant's path.
Advantages	**Advantages**
• Travels in all directions • Can be heard by animals that are hidden from view • Is useful for long-distance communication	• Builds a sense of belonging to the herd • Is silent so does not alert nearby animals to the elephant's presence

Did you know?

Elephants can produce sounds that are too low for people to hear. Such low sounds travel much further than higher sounds, enabling elephants to communicate over very long distances – up to 30 kilometres. Why would being able to communicate over such long distances help the elephants?

Smell

How

- The tip of an elephant's trunk is always on the move, looking for new smells.
- Elephants can tell if a member of their herd has passed through an area by smelling any urine left on the ground.
- Elephants also smell each other if they are ready to mate.

Advantages

- Needs little effort to smell, and the smell of urine remains on the ground for a long time

Movement

How

- An elephant shows it is **dominant** by trying to look larger, holding its head high above its shoulders, and spreading its ears.
- To show submission, an elephant carries its head low and its ears back.
- A frightened or excited elephant raises its tail and chin.

Advantages

- Nearby elephants can easily see whether an elephant is dominant, submissive or frightened.

17

▲ Bees collecting nectar

Dancing bees

For thousands of years, people have known that honey bees can communicate the location of food to each other. But it is only recently that we have been able to explain how this communication takes place.

In 1973, **zoologist** Dr Karl von Frisch won the Nobel Prize for his study of the honey bee. His work described how honey bees dance to show other bees in the hive where flowers containing nectar and pollen can be found.

Flowers containing nectar can be hard to find and each bee can carry only a small amount. If bees know where the nectar is, they don't have to spend time and energy searching for it.

Von Frisch observed how honey bees moved and he tracked them to see where the flowers were located. He developed a theory about how the dances worked.

He described two different honey bee dances: the round dance and the waggle dance. The round dance tells the location of flowers that are within about 50 metres of the hive. The waggle dance gives directions for finding flowers that are further away.

Bees at the entrance to a hive

The round dance

When performing the round dance, the honey bee turns in circles to the left and to the right. If there are many flowers, the bee communicates this by dancing more energetically and for longer. This dance does not tell which direction to fly. Instead, the other bees smell the flowers on the dancing bee and use this to find the flowers.

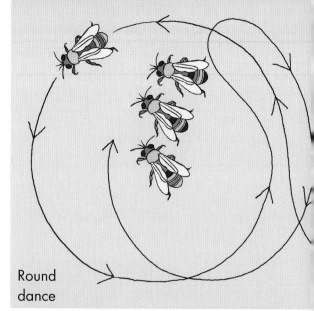

Round dance

The waggle dance

In the waggle dance, the honey bee moves in two loops with a straight part in between – much like a figure "8". The direction of the straight part of the dance tells the other bees which way to fly to the flowers. The speed at which the bee makes the loops and the amount of buzzing the bee does while dancing tell how far away the flowers are.

Not all scientists agree with von Frisch. They say that the "dances" exist, but they simply allow other bees to catch the scent of the flowers, which they then use to find the flowers.

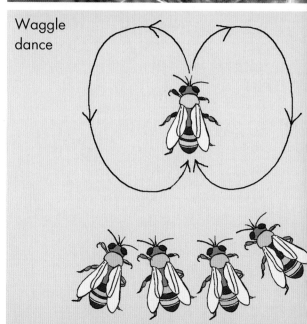

Waggle dance

Find out more

Find out more about bee communication:

- How does the queen bee communicate with other bees in her hive?

- What things do scout bees communicate?

Queen bee

Worker bees

Working together

Every bee **colony** depends on the bees cooperating with each other. Different bees do different jobs. Without good communication the colony would not survive.

There are three different types of bees in a honey bee hive:

- the queen bee – her only job is to lay thousands of eggs

- drone bees – these bees mate with the queen

- worker bees – these bees do all the work, including building the hive, feeding the queen, looking after the young bees, and collecting the nectar and pollen needed to make honey.

Chapter 4

Animals and language

Scientists want to find out whether animals are able to use **language**. They believe that learning about this will help us to better understand how humans develop language skills and whether animals are capable of **complex** thinking.

Scientists at the Ape Cognition and Conservation Initiative in Iowa, in the United States, have been training some bonobo chimpanzees to use language to communicate with humans.

Chimpanzees are not able to speak like people because they cannot make as many sounds as humans can. Instead the chimpanzees have been taught to use a keyboard that has symbols on it. The chimpanzee learns to associate a symbol with a particular thing. When the chimpanzee points to the symbol, or presses the key, it is thought to be communicating with its trainer. The scientists have videos that show these animals using sign language to make simple sentences.

One day, one of the chimpanzees called Panbanisha made some hand signs that scientists understood to be the words "fight", "mad" and "Austin". It was found that during the night another chimpanzee called Austin had been involved in a noisy fight with his mother, which Panbanisha had overheard. The scientists working with the chimp believed that Panbanisha was trying to tell them about this.

What is language?

Language is any system of symbols that is used to communicate meaning. These symbols can be sounds (such as spoken words), finger and hand movements (such as sign language) and text marks (such as written words and numbers).

 Find out more

What have the bonobos at the Ape Cognition and Conservation Initiative been doing lately? What does this tell us about animals and their ability to use language?

Kanzi and his trainer, scientist
Dr Sue Savage-Rumbaugh

 **Did
you
know?**

"Kanzi" means "treasure".
It is a word from an African
language called Swahili.

Meet Kanzi

Kanzi is another bonobo chimpanzee that lives at
the Ape Cognition and Conservation Initiative. The
scientists who work with Kanzi say that he is able to
understand spoken language and to communicate his
thoughts using a set of symbols. They believe that
Kanzi can understand about 500 words.

Kanzi has also shown that he can match the correct symbols to words he hears in headphones.

He listens to the word, then points to the real object, the photo, or the symbol that the word represents.

Kanzi learned a lot of language when he was very young. He learned by listening in on lessons his adoptive mother was getting.

Kanzi can also make simple stone tools that are sharp enough to cut through **hide** or rope. He is able to build a fire, light it using matches and cook food such as omelette and marshmallows on the fire. When he has finished, he pours water on the fire to put it out.

Kanzi has been taught to communicate.

Sign language

People who cannot speak can communicate using a system of hand and finger gestures called sign language. Different sign languages are used in different countries.

People who cannot speak or use sign language may communicate using small computerised keyboards that use pictures and symbols, similar to those used by the chimpanzees.

Australian Sign Language (Auslan)

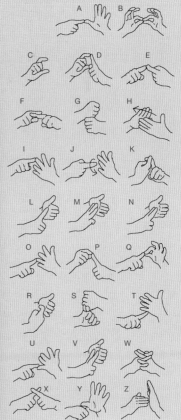

25

Can animals really use language?

There has been a great deal of debate among scientists about whether animals can learn to use language, and there are differing points of view.

Animals cannot use language

Humans are the only living things that can use language. No other animals have brains that are able to create and understand language, and this amazing ability makes humans different from animals. Trying to teach animals to talk is like trying to teach humans to fly.

Animals do not have the vocal cords to make the sounds of language nor do they have the brain structure to learn how to communicate using language.

Animals that seem to understand what humans are saying are just very good at understanding the tone of voice or the facial expression the human is showing.

Animals can use language

There is a growing amount of evidence that animals can learn to use language. Animals such as chimpanzees and orangutans have been taught to communicate using keyboards, sign language and even computers to make simple sentences. Animals have shown that they can learn symbols for words, and that they can then put these symbols together to create simple messages.

There are a range of examples that demonstrate this. For example, during one experiment an ape was asked, "Are you a human or a gorilla?" The gorilla responded by using signs that communicated the message "Fine animal gorilla". This is the same type of language used by a two-year-old child who says "Up, Mummy" to let her mother know that she wants to be picked up. If we accept that the child is using language, then we must also agree that the gorilla is using language.

Find out more

Can you find examples where chimpanzees have combined signs to make new words?

What does "using language" mean?

Perhaps one of the reasons scientists do not agree is that they do not mean the same thing when they say "using language". If an animal must use complex sentences and proper grammar to be said to be using language, then it is true that animals do not use language. If, on the other hand, simple messages of two or three words are accepted as language, then there is a lot of evidence that some animals do use language.

How is language learned?

When a human baby is born, it cries to signal it wants food, warmth and comfort. This crying is called an instinct – the baby has not learned to cry, rather it is a natural behaviour. As the baby gets older, it uses language to ask, "May I have my breakfast, please?" Children learn to use language by being taught to speak by people around them and by copying how other people talk.

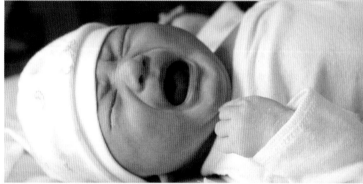

Conclusion

As scientists continue to study animal communication, we are likely to find out more about different kinds of animals and learn more about how these animals' brains work. This may help us to understand these animals better.

Learning more about how animals communicate may also help us to understand more about how and why humans have developed the ability to use language.

Glossary

body language the way the body can be used to communicate without talking

cells tiny units of the body

colony a large group of the same sort of animal living together

complex made up of many parts that are linked

dominant having the highest position in the group; often the biggest or most powerful male animal in a group

fertilise to add sperm to the eggs to make them grow

habitat a plant or animal's natural environment

hide an animal skin

language a system of symbols used to communicate meaning

mottled spotted with different colours

predator an animal that kills and eats other animals

socialise to be with others

species a group of living things that can reproduce with each other, but not with another group or species

territories areas that animals see as their own

zoologist a scientist who studies animals

Index